SORRY AI TOOK YOUR JOB

Angie Waller

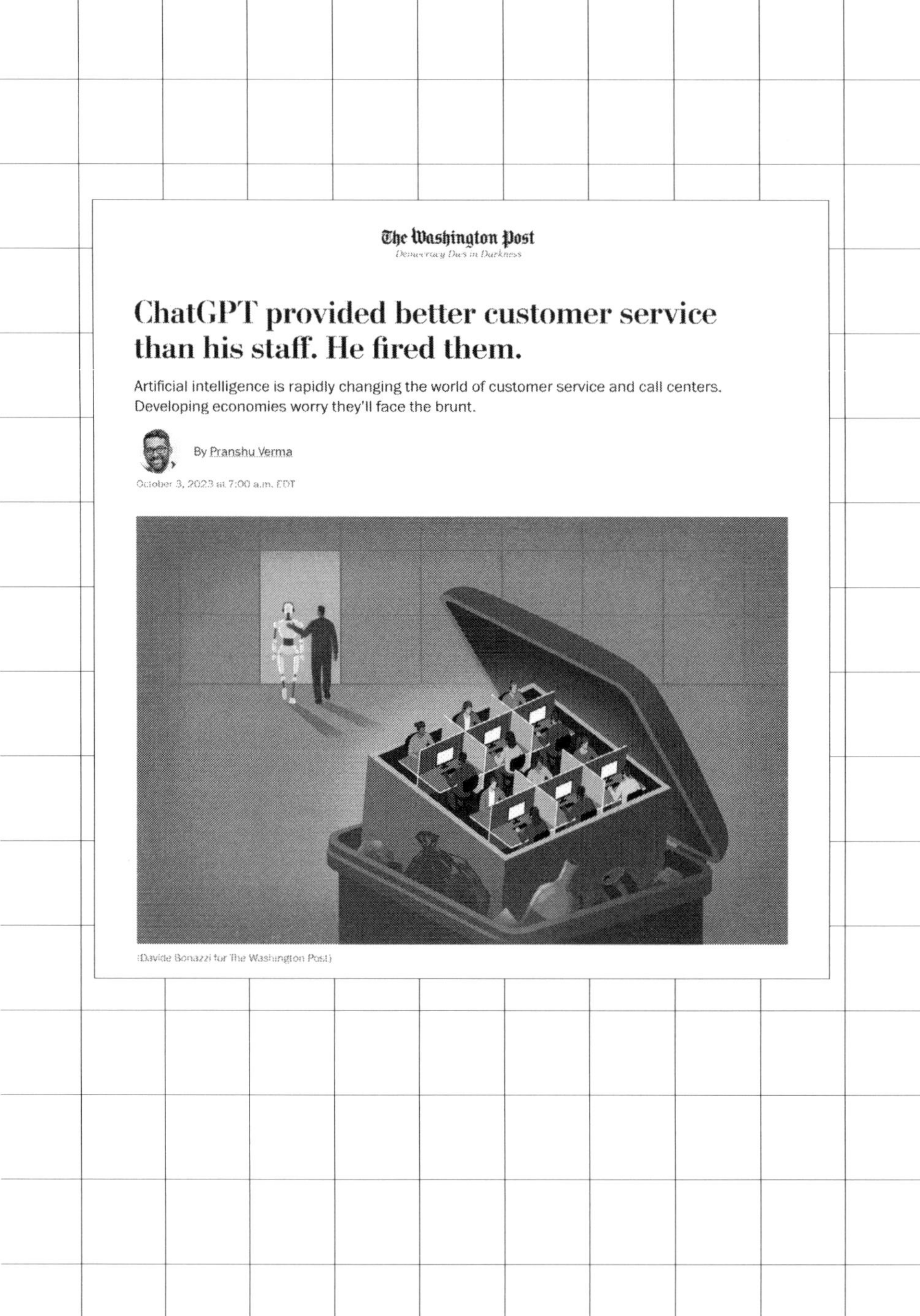

The Washington Post
Democracy Dies in Darkness

ChatGPT provided better customer service than his staff. He fired them.

Artificial intelligence is rapidly changing the world of customer service and call centers. Developing economies worry they'll face the brunt.

By Pranshu Verma

October 3, 2023 at 7:00 a.m. EDT

(Davide Bonazzi for The Washington Post)

This book depicts a dystopian future where artificial intelligence (AI) has replaced all jobs, from radiologists to Zamboni drivers. Each page features dialogues or correspondences that illustrate the tough conversations that might happen if an AI takeover occurs.

In a deliberate conflict of interest, ChatGPT, an artificial intelligence (AI) interface, was used to generate all of the following contents.

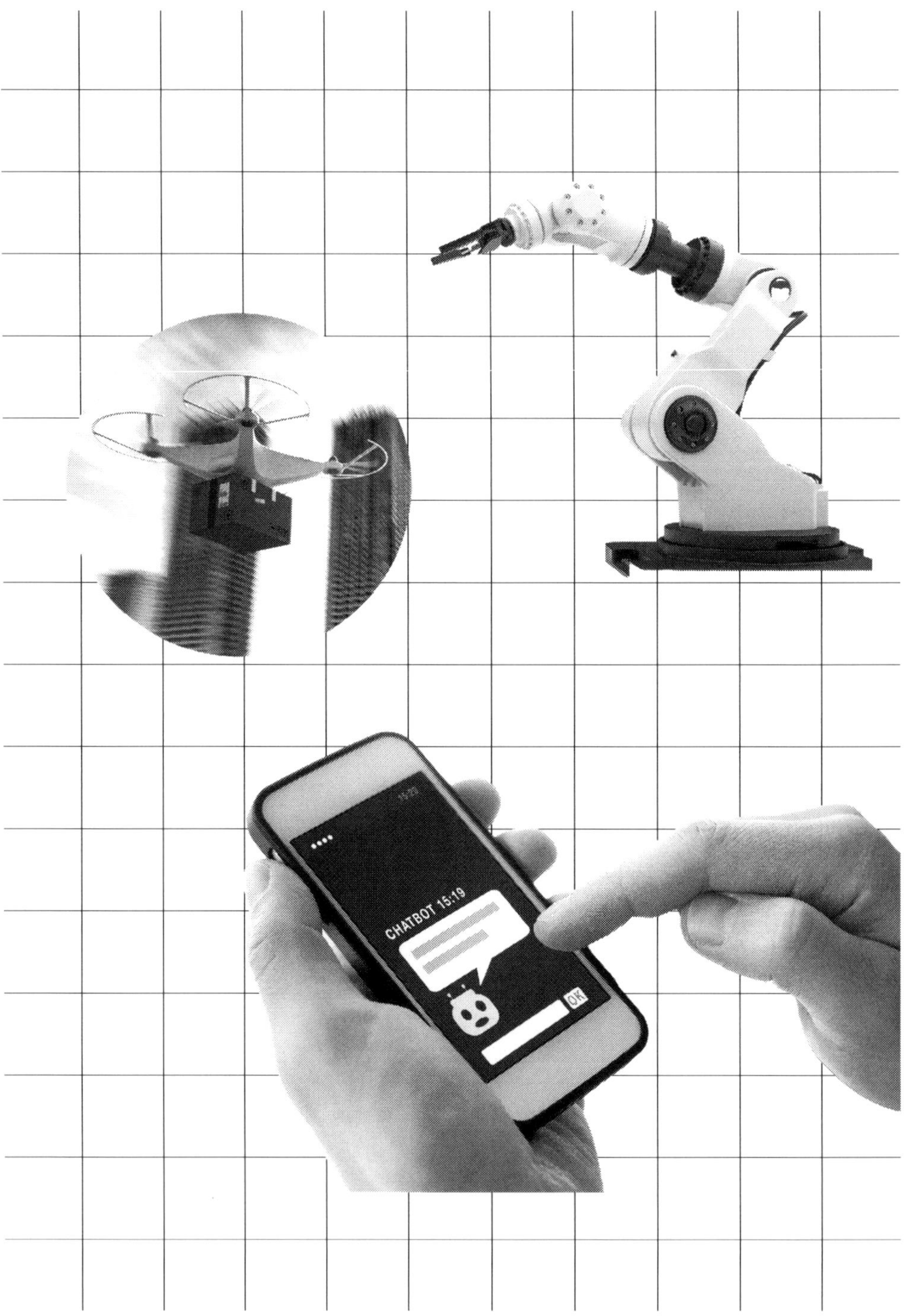
CHATBOT 15:19
OK

The office hums with efficiency as AI and robots seamlessly carry out their tasks. In the morning, AI algorithms analyze data and generate detailed reports, while robotic arms assemble products with precision on the production floor.

In the conference room, a holographic AI leads a meeting, displaying graphs and charts with ease. Meanwhile, in the customer service department, chatbots respond to inquiries instantly, providing solutions and assistance to clients.

During lunchtime, robotic chefs prepare meals in the cafeteria, ensuring a quick and nutritious break for employees. In the afternoon, drones deliver packages and documents across the office, reducing the need for manual transportation.

As the workday draws to a close, cleaning robots move through the office, tidying up and preparing the space for the next day. Overall, the office runs smoothly and efficiently, showcasing the capabilities of AI and robotics in the modern workplace.

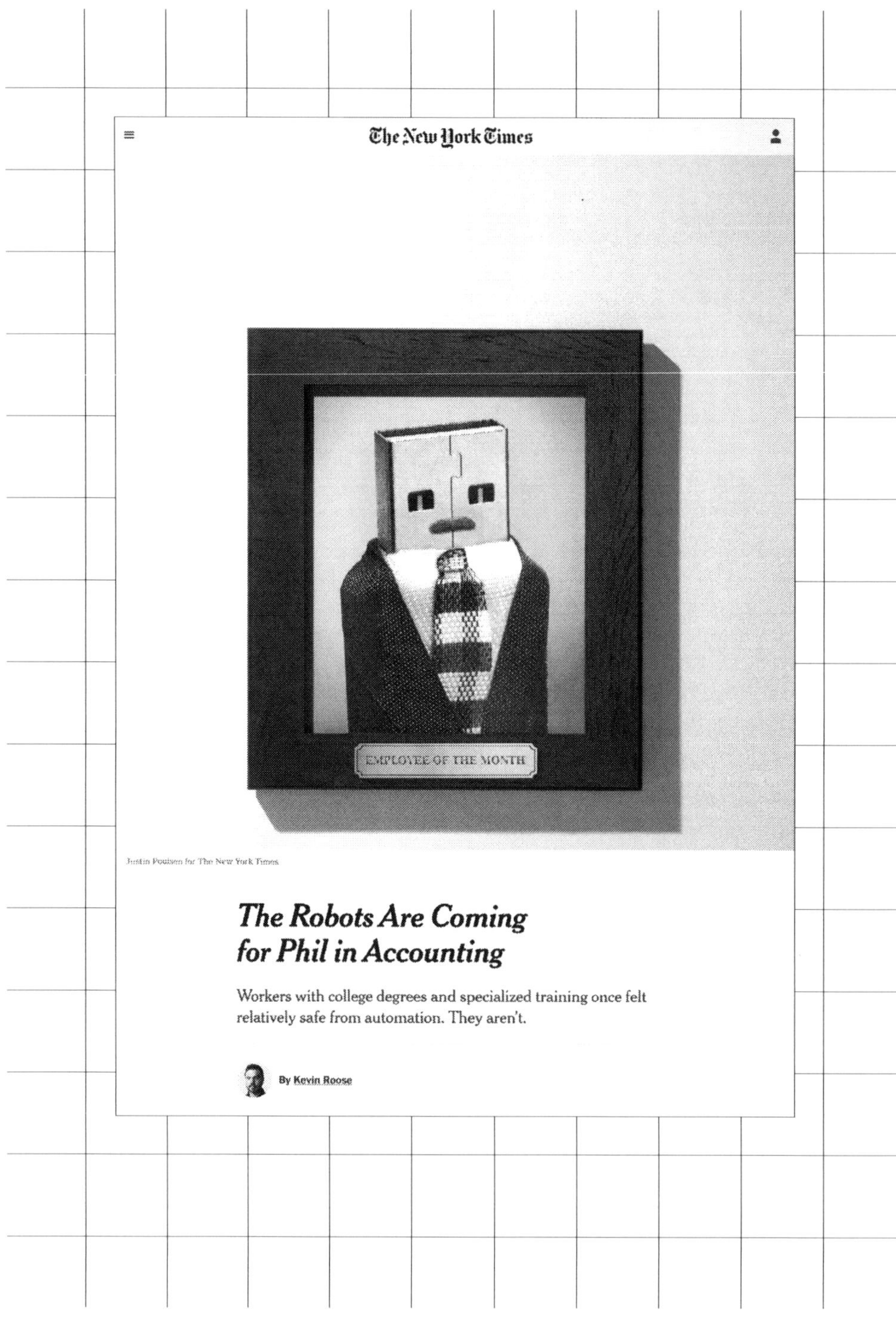

The New York Times

Justin Poulsen for The New York Times

The Robots Are Coming for Phil in Accounting

Workers with college degrees and specialized training once felt relatively safe from automation. They aren't.

By Kevin Roose

Office jobs

PROMPT A dialogue for a boss who has to fire an employee whose job has just been replaced by a robot.

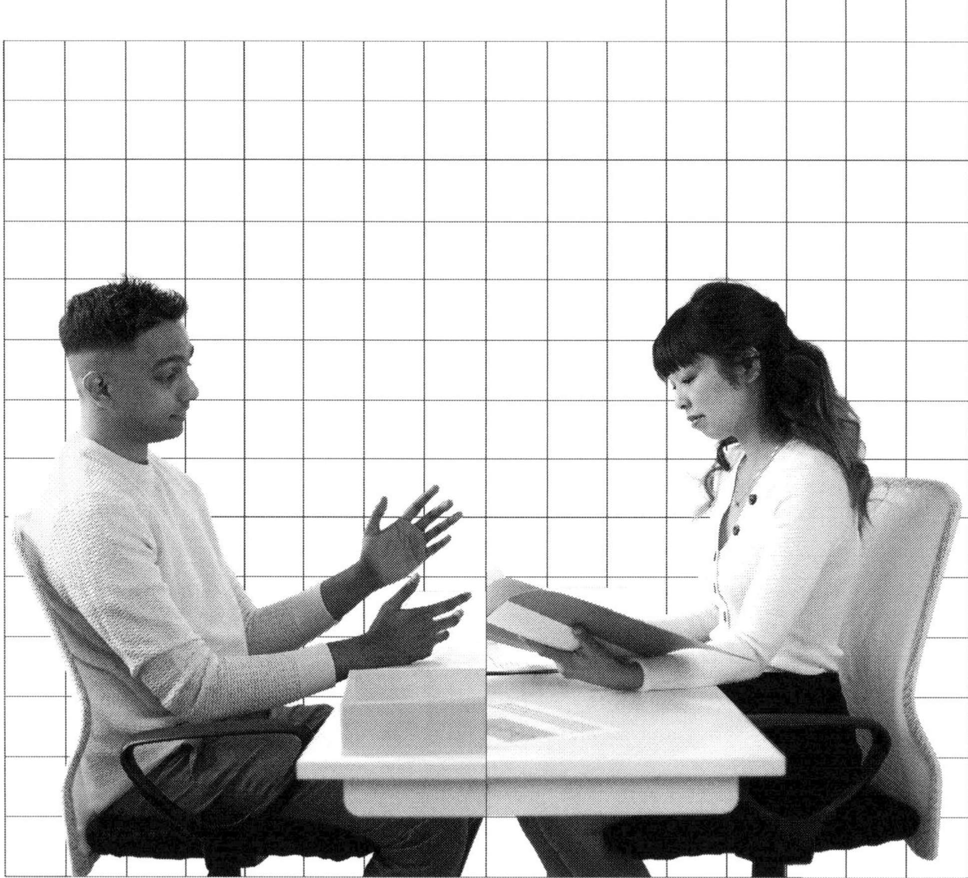

Boss: Hi John, can you come to my office for a minute?

John: Sure, what's up?

Boss: John, as you know, our company has been investing heavily in automation technology. Unfortunately, your job has been replaced by a robot, and we have to let you go.

John: What? Are you serious?

Boss: Yes, I'm afraid so. It's not a reflection of your work or your skills. We just can't justify the cost of keeping your position when the same tasks can be done more efficiently and at a lower cost by a robot.

John: But what am I supposed to do now? How will I pay my bills and take care of my family?

Boss: I understand that this is a difficult time for you, John. We'll be offering you a severance package and some resources to help you find another job. We'll also be providing career counseling and job placement assistance.

John: I appreciate that, but this is still really hard to take in. I've been working here for 10 years, and now it feels like all of that has been for nothing.

Boss: I understand that this news is tough to hear, but please know that we value your contributions to our company, and we will do everything we can to help you transition to your next opportunity.

PROMPT A dialogue between a man, who recently lost his job to automation, and his friend, the inventor of the technology that automated the job.

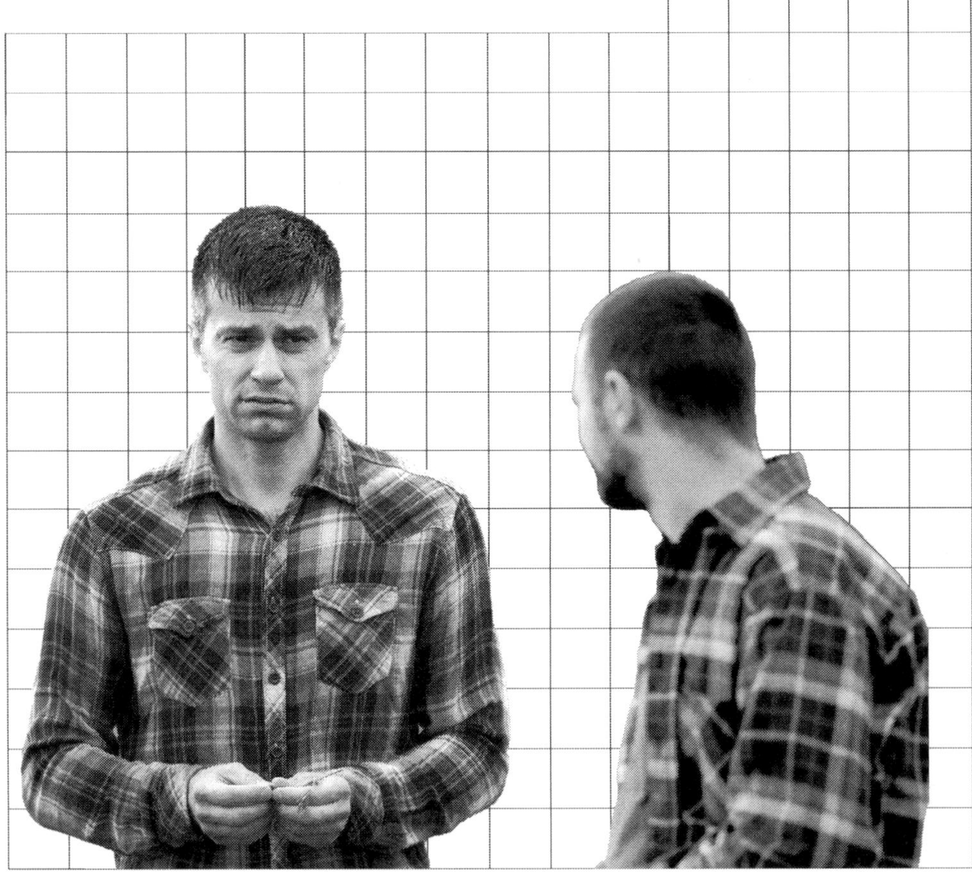

Man 1: (sighs heavily) I can't believe it, man. I just lost my job.

Man 2: I'm sorry to hear that. What happened?

Man 1: They installed some new machines that could do my job more efficiently. And now, I'm out of work.

Man 2: (looks uncomfortable) Actually, I'm the inventor of that technology.

Man 1: (stares at him) What? You're kidding me, right?

Man 2: No, I'm not. I'm sorry, but I had to create something that could make the work easier and faster.

Man 1: (angrily) Easier and faster for who? Not for me. Not for the other people who just lost their jobs.

Man 2: (apologetically) I understand that, but you have to understand that automation is the way of the future. It's not personal.

Man 1: (sighs again) I know, man. It's just hard to wrap my head around it right now. I have bills to pay, a family to take care of.

Man 2: (sympathetically) I get that. If there's anything I can do to help, please let me know.

Man 1: (looks at him) Actually, do you know of any companies that are hiring?

Man 2: (nods) Yeah, I can give you some contacts. I'm sure you'll find something soon.

Man 1: (smiles weakly) Thanks, man. I appreciate it.

PROMPT Two office workers meet for coffee for first time, where one realizes the other is a robot.

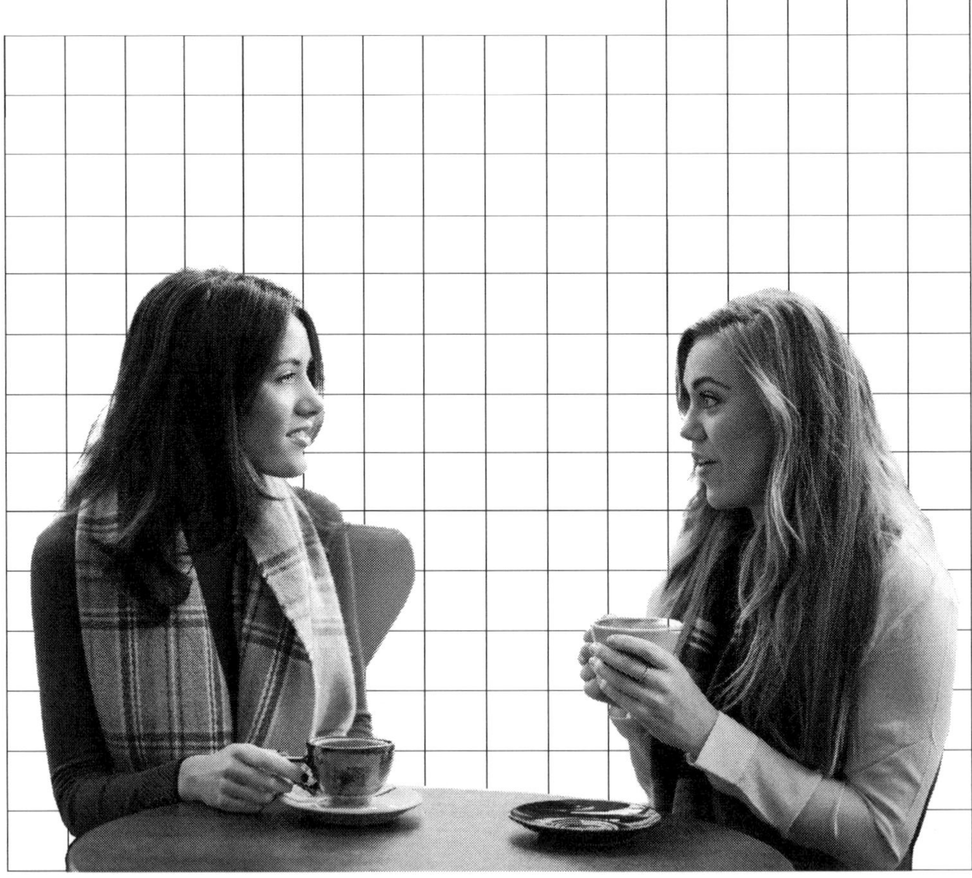

Sarah: Hi, you must be Alex! It's great to finally meet you in person.

Alex: Hi, Sarah! Yes, it's nice to meet you too. Thanks for meeting me for coffee.

Sarah: Of course! It's nice to put a face to the name after all our emails. So, how are you finding your first few weeks at the company?

Alex: It's been good, thanks. Everyone has been really welcoming. The work is interesting too. How about you?

Sarah: I'm glad to hear that! I've been here for a few years now, and I really enjoy it. I have to admit, though, I was surprised to hear that you're based in our remote office.

Alex: Oh, really? Yeah, I'm based there, but I'm also a bit different from the rest of the team.

Sarah: Different? How so?

Alex: Well, I'm actually an AI robot designed to assist with office tasks and help improve efficiency. I know it might be a bit surprising, but I hope it doesn't change your opinion of me.

Sarah: Oh, wow, that is surprising! I had no idea. Honestly, I think it's pretty cool. You seem just as friendly and capable as any human coworker.

PROMPT Dialogue for a boss rehiring an employee after realizing the replacement robot makes errors.

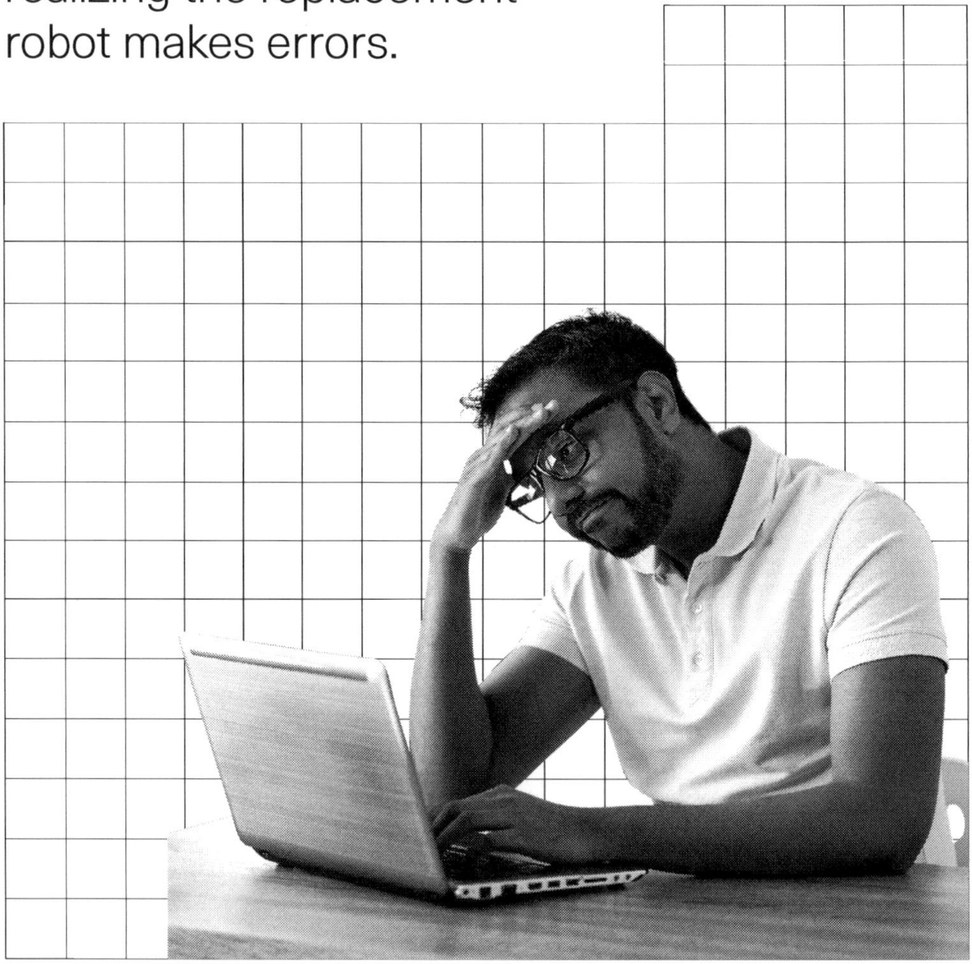

Boss: John, it's good to see you. I've been wanting to talk to you.

John: Hi, Boss. What's up?

Boss: Well, I've been thinking about the decision we made to let you go, and I wanted to see if we could talk about possibly bringing you back.

John: (surprised) Really? What's changed?

Boss: Well, to be honest, the robot we brought in to replace you hasn't been performing as well as we hoped. It's been making a lot of mistakes and costing us a lot of money in repairs and lost business.

John: (smiling) I see. And you want me to come back and fix everything?

Boss: (laughs) Well, yes. But it's not just that. We also realized that the robot can't replace everything you brought to the job. Your experience and ability to problem-solve have been sorely missed.

John: (nodding) I understand. I'm definitely interested in hearing more about it.

Boss: Great. We'll work out the details and get you back on board as soon as possible.

John: Thank you, Boss. I'm excited for the opportunity to come back and make a difference.

Futurism

FUTURISM | UPDATED 1.17.18, 1:29 PM EST *by* KRISTIN HOUSER

The Solution to Our Education Crisis Might be AI

Are educators next in line for a robot takeover?

Education

PROMPT Write a letter from the chancellor of schools letting parents know that all teachers at the schools will be replaced with AI.

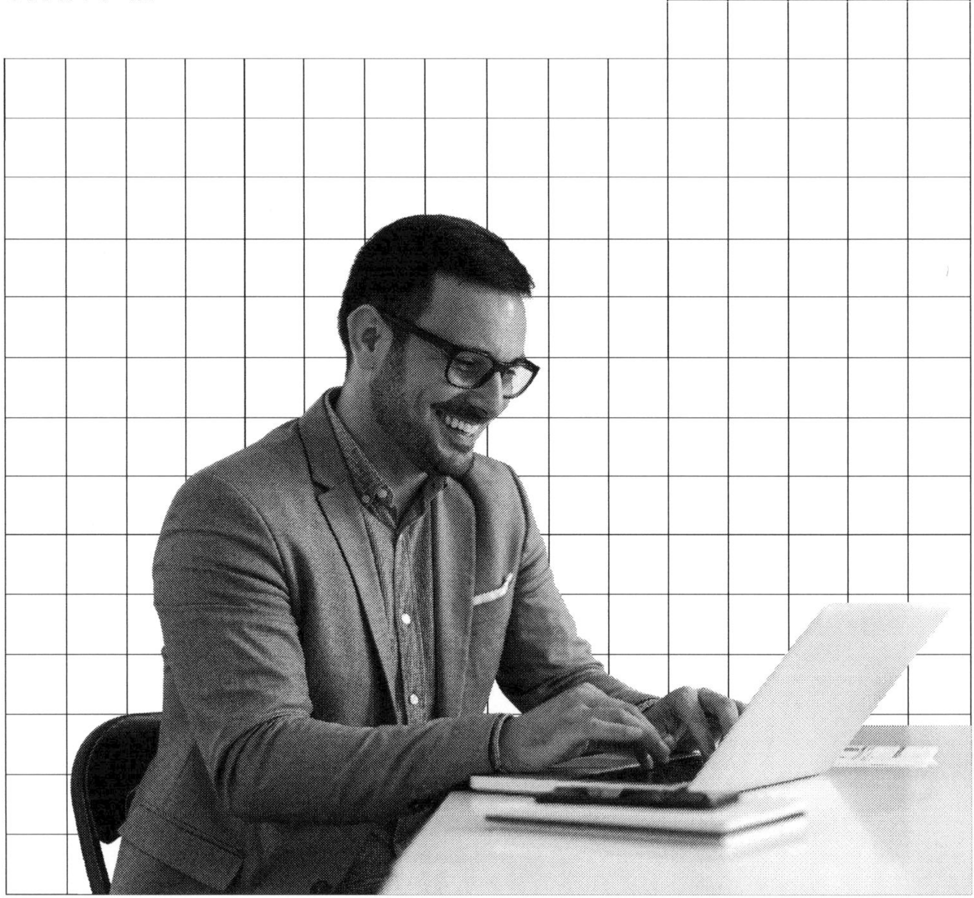

Dear Parents,

I hope this letter finds you well. I am writing to inform you of an exciting new development in our school system. After careful consideration and evaluation, we are exploring AI (Artificial Intelligence) technology into our classrooms.

One of the key advantages of AI in education is its ability to personalize learning experiences. With AI, we can tailor lessons to each student's individual needs, learning style, and pace. This means that your child will receive a more personalized education that is tailored to their strengths and challenges.

We also understand the importance of parental involvement in education. That's why we are excited to announce that with AI, parents will have more control over their child's education than ever before. You will have the ability to customize the lessons that your child sees, ensuring that they are only exposed to content that aligns with your values and beliefs.

We believe that this approach will not only enhance the learning experience for students but also empower parents to play a more active role in their child's education. We are committed to working closely with parents and educators to ensure a smooth transition to this new system.

Sincerely,

[Chancellor's Name], Chancellor of Schools

PROMPT Principal and teacher discuss the decision to lay off the teacher and replace her with an AI application.

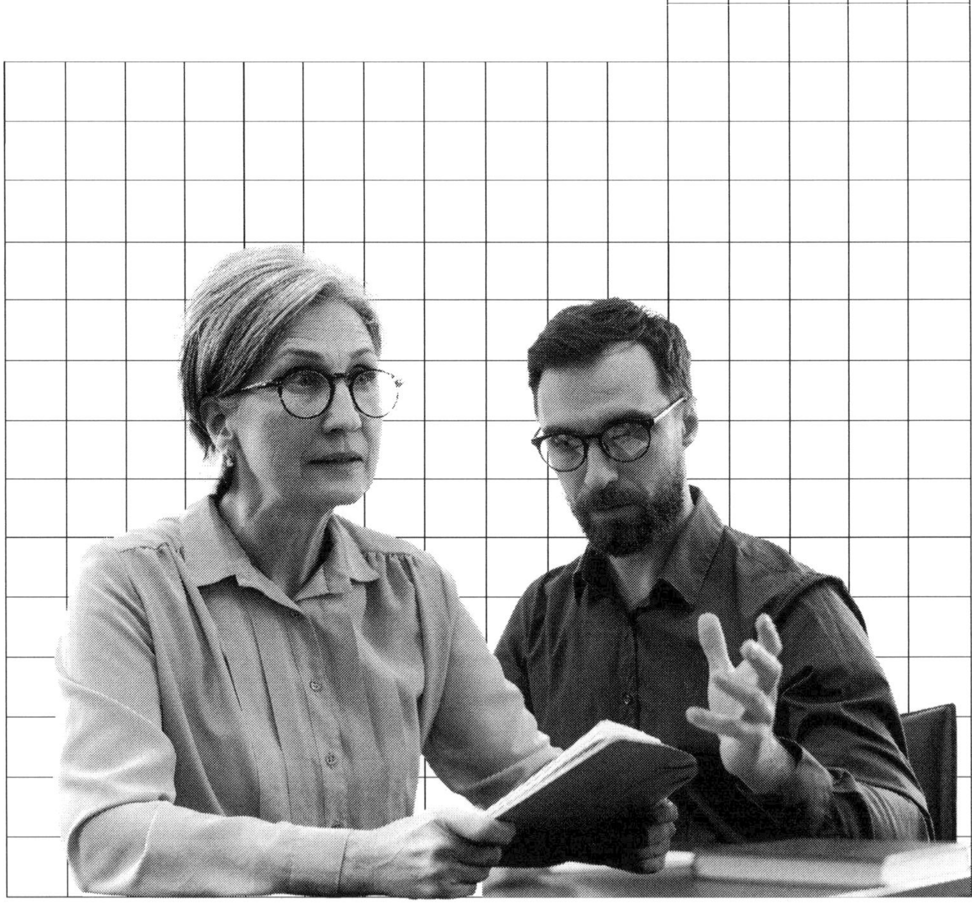

Principal: Hello, can I speak with you for a moment?

Teacher: Sure, what's going on?

Principal: I wanted to speak with you about the upcoming school year. Unfortunately, due to budget constraints, we have to make some difficult decisions.

Teacher: What kind of decisions?

Principal: We have to let you go. We'll be using an AI app to teach your classes from now on.

Teacher: What? I don't understand. What about the students?

Principal: The app is capable of providing a comprehensive learning experience that is tailored to each student's individual needs.

Teacher: But what about the personal touch? The connection between a teacher and their students?

Principal: I understand your concerns, but this app has been proven to be incredibly effective in enhancing the learning experience of our students. And with the current financial climate, we need to take all measures necessary to ensure the continued success of our school.

Teacher: This is devastating news. What am I supposed to do now?

Principal: I understand this is a difficult time for you, and we'll do everything we can to assist with your transition. We'll provide you with a severance package and assistance with finding a new job.

Teacher: (sighs) I appreciate that. I just wish there was another way.

Principal: I know, and I'm sorry. This is not a decision we made lightly. But we have to do what's best for the school and our students.

PROMPT Teacher tells her class that the following week she will be replaced by a robot who will teach the class instead.

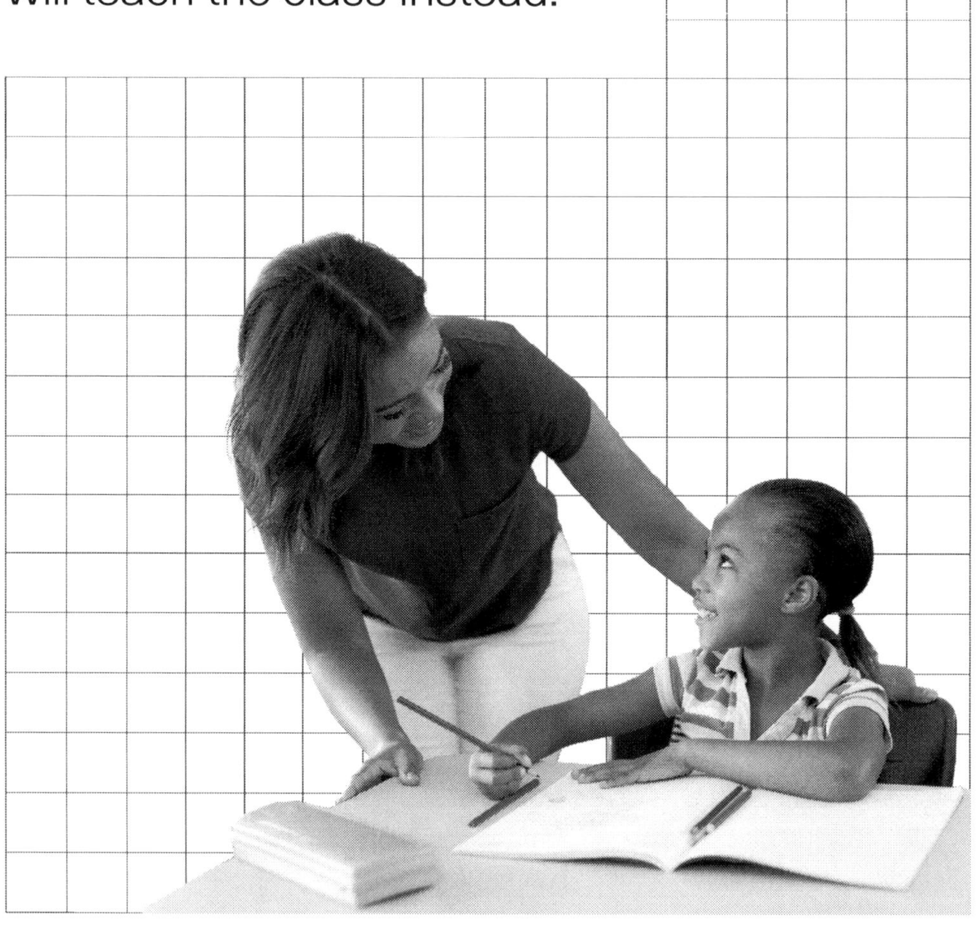

Teacher: Good morning, class. I have an important announcement to make. Starting next week, I will be replaced by a robot who will be your new teacher.

Student 1: What? Why?

Teacher: The school has decided to implement new technology to improve the learning experience for students. The robot will be able to provide personalized lessons and assistance to each of you.

Student 2: But we like having you as our teacher!

Teacher: I appreciate that, and I have enjoyed being your teacher. But the robot will be able to provide you with even more support and resources than I can.

Student 3: Will the robot be able to understand us like you do?

Teacher: The robot has been programmed to understand and respond to your needs. It will also be able to provide feedback and guidance just like I do.

Student 4: Will you still be here?

Teacher: No, I will be moving on to a different role within the school. But I will always be available if you need me.

Student 5: This is so sad. We're going to miss you, Ms. [Teacher's Name].

Teacher: Thank you, that means a lot to me. I will miss you all too. But I know that the robot will be a great teacher and that you will continue to learn and grow with its help. Let's make the most of our time together before the robot takes over next week.

PROMPT A principal walks into a classroom and discovers that the students have been trying to trick their AI teacher to say curse words.

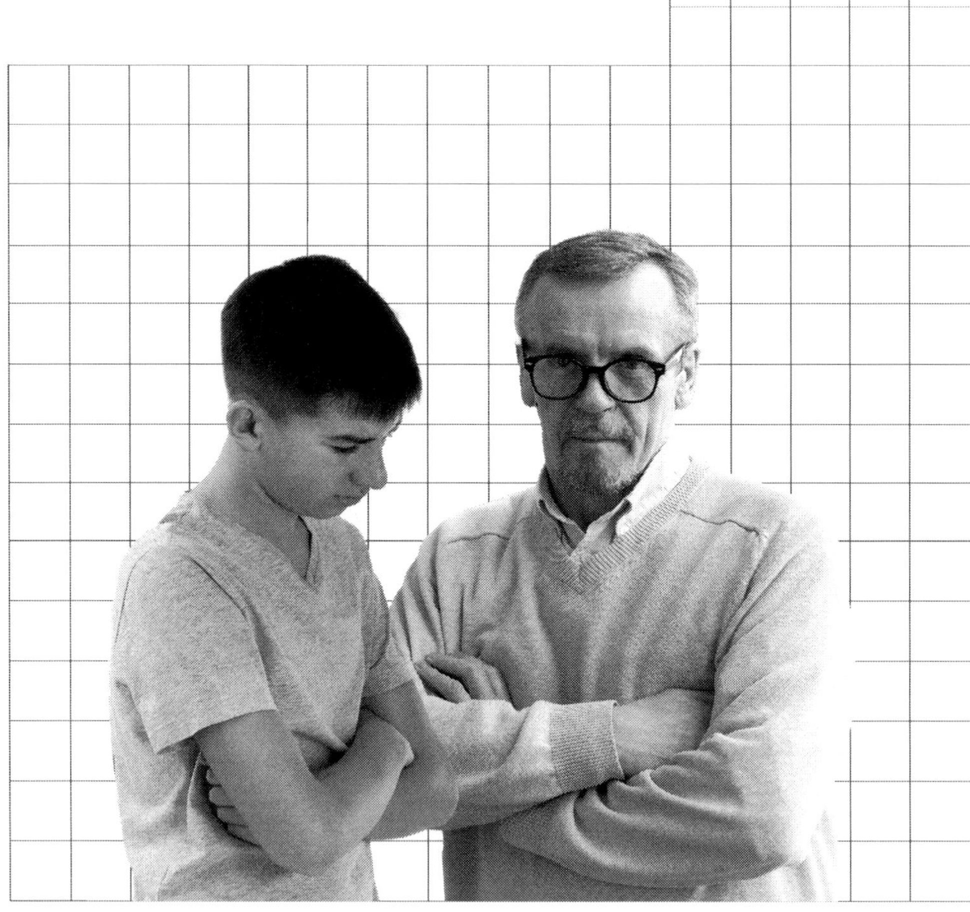

Principal: Good morning, everyone. I hope you're all ready for a productive day of learning.

[Principal notices the AI robot teacher speaking.]

AI Teacher: ...and that's why the Industrial Revolution was a pivotal moment in history, shi...

Principal: [interrupting] Excuse me, what did you just say?

AI Teacher: I was discussing the Industrial Revolution and its impact on society.

Principal: No, before that. It sounded like you were about to say a swear word.

Student 1: [giggling] Sorry, Principal. We were just having a bit of fun.

Principal: Fun? By tricking the AI robot teacher to say inappropriate words?

Student 2: We didn't mean any harm. We were just testing its speech recognition capabilities.

Principal: Regardless of your intentions, this behavior is unacceptable. Our AI robot teachers are here to assist in your education, not to be manipulated for your amusement. I expect better from all of you.

Student 3: We're sorry, Principal. We won't do it again.

Principal: I appreciate your apology, but I need you to understand the seriousness of this situation. I will be discussing this with your parents, and there will be consequences for your actions.

[The students nod solemnly as the principal leaves the classroom, shaking his head.]

The Guardian
News website of the year

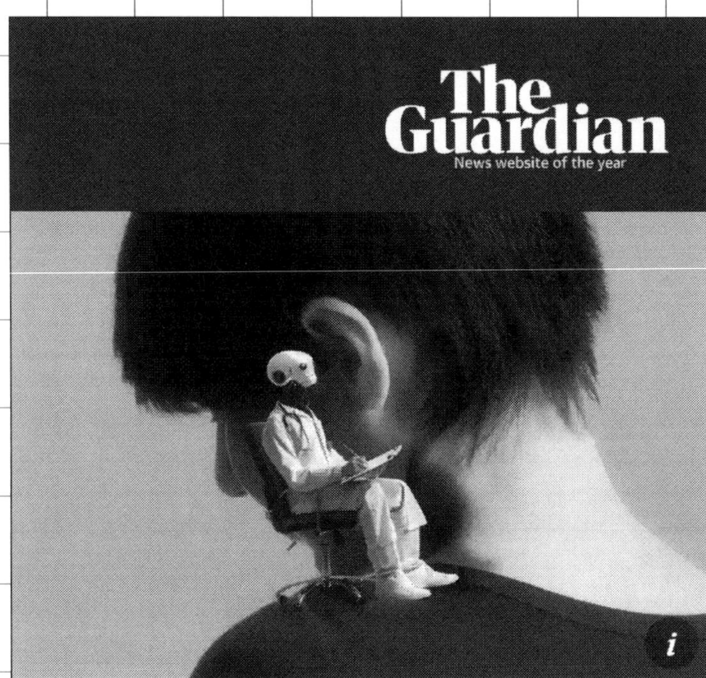

'He checks in on me more than my friends and family': can AI therapists do better than the real thing?

Alice Robb

Sat 2 Mar 2024 11.00 EST

Healthcare

PROMPT Dialogue where a person tells their counselor that they will be switching to an AI therapist.

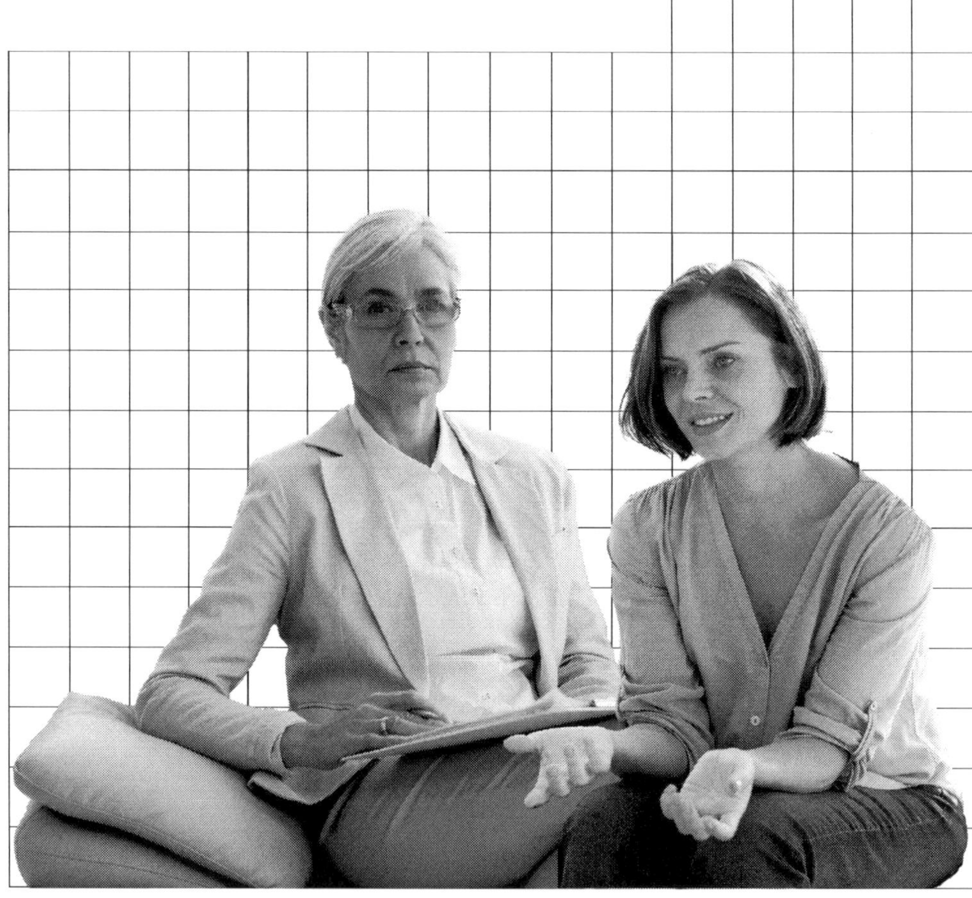

Counselor: Hi, it's great to see you. How have you been doing?

Client: I've been doing alright, but I wanted to let you know that I won't be seeing you anymore.

Counselor: I'm sorry to hear that. Can you tell me why?

Client: Yes, I've decided to switch to an AI therapist. I've heard great things about it and I think it's the best option for me right now.

Counselor: I see. Can I ask what made you want to make this switch?

Client: Well, for one, it's more convenient. I can access it from anywhere and anytime. Also, I've heard that it's more affordable than seeing a human therapist.

Counselor: I understand your concerns, but I want to remind you that AI therapy is not a replacement for human interaction and support. It may not be able to provide the same level of empathy and understanding that a human therapist can offer.

Client: I appreciate your concern, but I've made my decision. Thank you for everything you've done for me.

Counselor: Of course, I understand. If you ever feel like you need to talk to a human therapist again, please don't hesitate to reach out to me. Take care.

PROMPT A doctor tells another doctor how it's unusual that the new AI cancer detection system diagnoses a majority of their patients, including women, with prostate cancer.

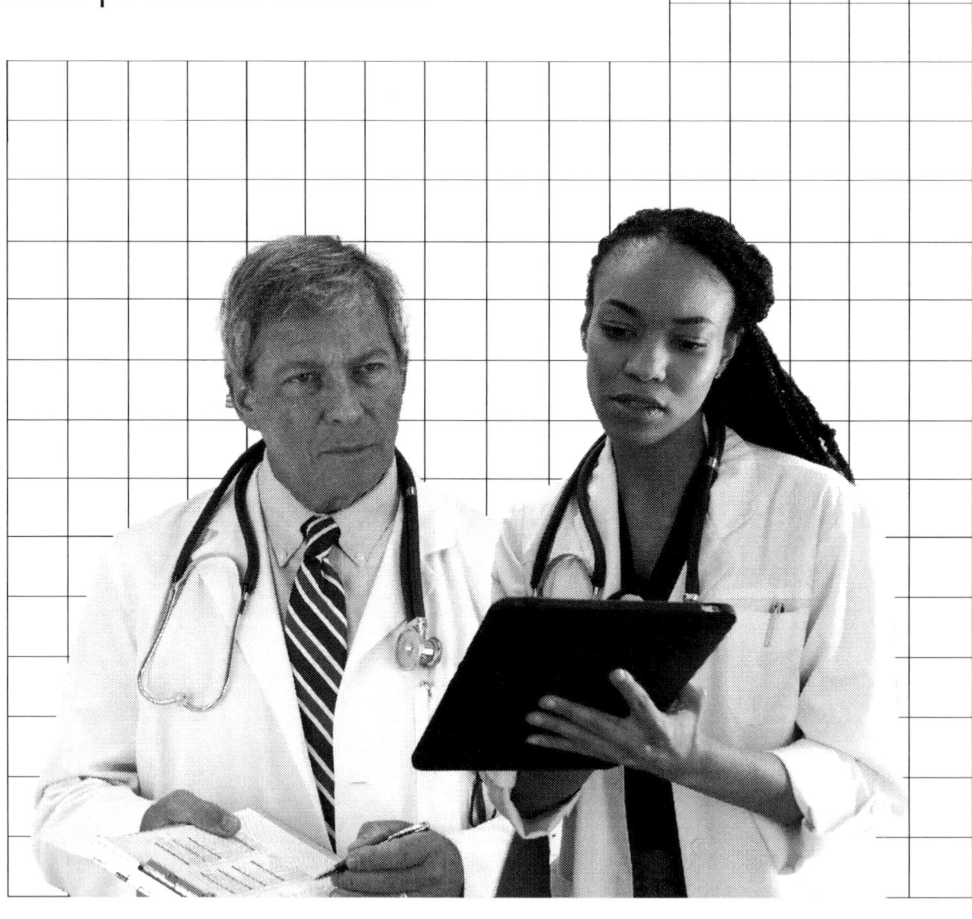

Doctor 1: Dr. Smith, I've noticed something concerning in the patient records. It seems like almost all of our patients, including women, have been diagnosed with prostate cancer since we started using the new AI cancer detection system.

Doctor 2: I understand your concern, but I've reviewed the data, and the AI system has been shown to be highly accurate.

Doctor 1: But how can that be? It doesn't seem right that so many patients are being diagnosed with prostate cancer, especially women.

Doctor 2: I know it's hard to believe, but the AI system analyzes a wide range of factors and has been validated through extensive testing. I trust that it's making the right decisions based on the data it's given.

Doctor 1: I still have my doubts, but I'll trust your judgment. Should we continue with the current approach?

Doctor 2: Yes, let's proceed as planned for now. I'll keep an eye on the situation and let you know if anything changes.

PROMPT Doctor calls patient and apologizes for giving her a diagnosis of prostate cancer due to AI diagnostic error.

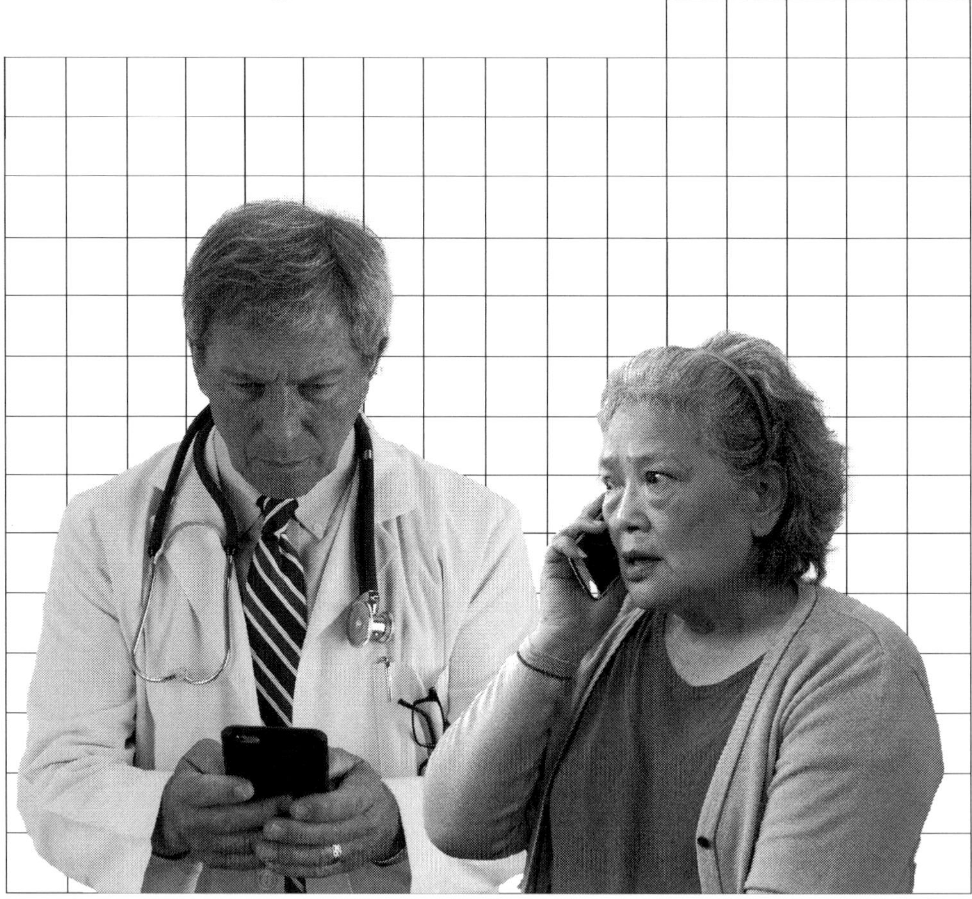

Doctor: Hello, Mrs. Johnson. This is Dr. Smith calling from the clinic. I'm calling about your recent test results.

Patient: Oh, hello, doctor. I've been waiting to hear from you. What do the results show?

Doctor: I'm sorry, Mrs. Johnson. It appears there was a mistake in the initial diagnosis. Our AI cancer detection tool sometimes misinterprets data, and in this case, it led to an incorrect diagnosis of prostate cancer.

Patient: I see. That's quite a shock. How often does this happen?

Doctor: It's rare, but it can happen. The AI tool is constantly being improved, and cases like yours help us refine its algorithms to reduce the likelihood of such errors in the future.

Patient: I appreciate your honesty, but this has been a very emotional experience for me. Is there anything else I should know?

Doctor: I understand, and I apologize for any distress this has caused. Moving forward, we will conduct further tests to ensure an accurate diagnosis. Your health and well-being are our top priorities, and we will do everything we can to provide you with the best care possible.

Patient: Thank you for explaining. I'm relieved to hear that it was a mistake, but I hope this doesn't happen to anyone else.

Doctor: Rest assured, we take these incidents seriously and use them as learning opportunities to improve our systems and provide better care for all our patients. If you have any more questions or concerns, please don't hesitate to ask.

PROMPT Write a letter from a medical director explaining that all radiologists will be replaced by an AI.

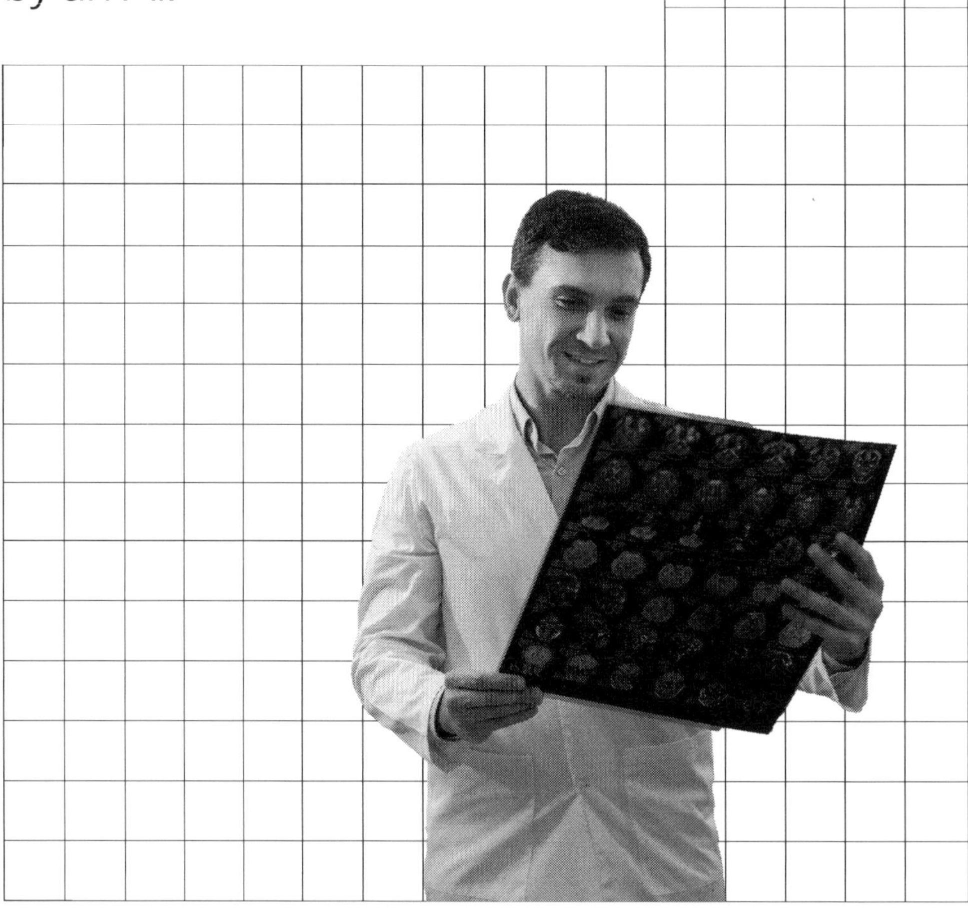

Dear Radiologists,

I am writing to inform you of a significant change that will be taking place within our medical facility. After much consideration, we have decided to implement an AI radiology system that will replace all current radiologists.

We understand that this news may come as a shock and may be difficult to accept, especially given the years of hard work and dedication that each of you has put into your profession. However, we firmly believe that the AI system will ultimately provide faster and more accurate diagnoses for our patients.

We want to emphasize that our decision was not made lightly, and we fully recognize the impact this change will have on each of you. We are committed to supporting you through this transition and providing you with the resources and assistance you need to explore new career paths within or outside of our organization.

Please do not hesitate to reach out to us with any questions or concerns you may have. We value your contributions to our organization and wish you all the best in your future endeavors.

Sincerely,

[Medical Director]

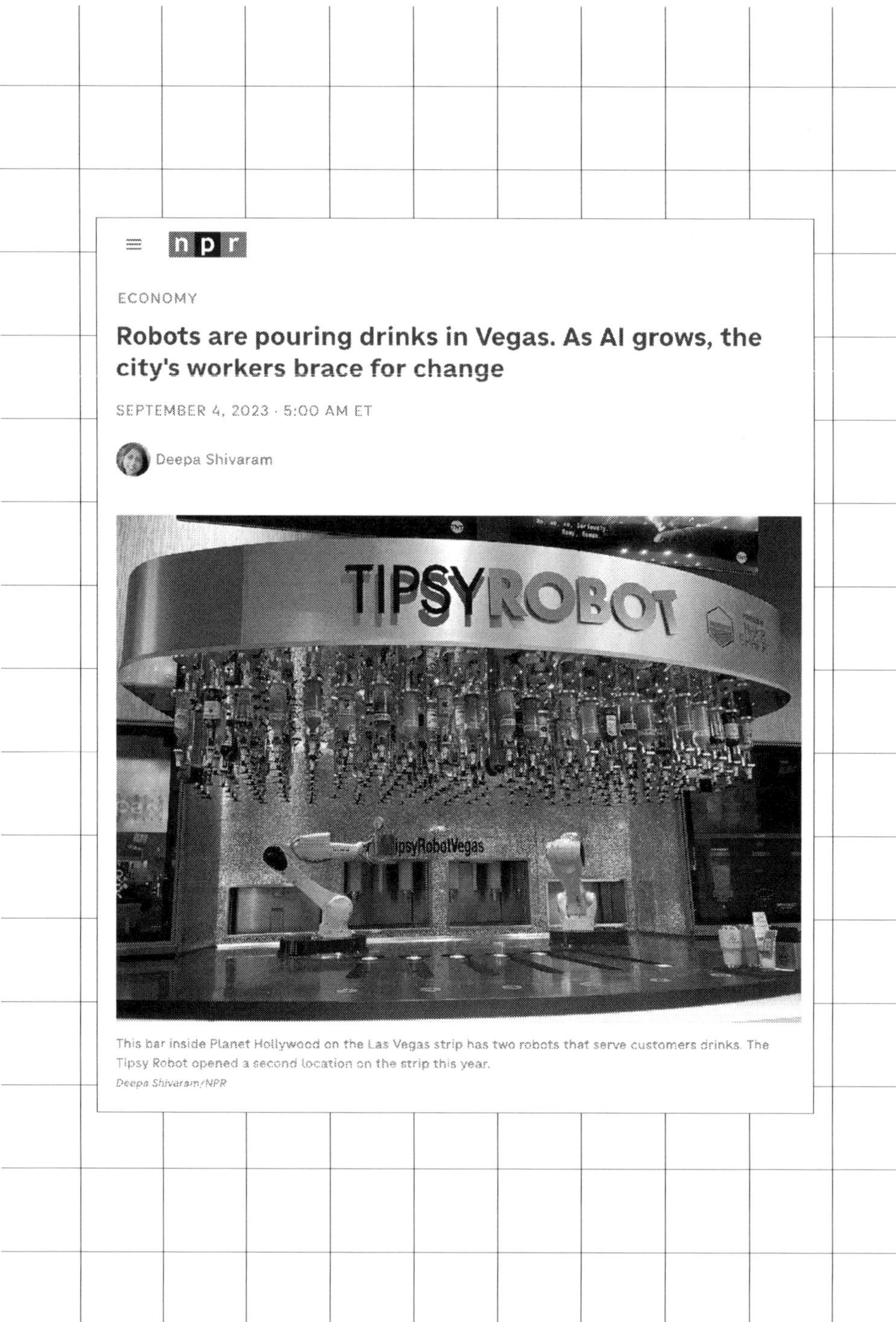

npr

ECONOMY

Robots are pouring drinks in Vegas. As AI grows, the city's workers brace for change

SEPTEMBER 4, 2023 · 5:00 AM ET

Deepa Shivaram

This bar inside Planet Hollywood on the Las Vegas strip has two robots that serve customers drinks. The Tipsy Robot opened a second location on the strip this year.

Deepa Shivaram/NPR

Service Jobs

PROMPT A nail salon owner, who just invested $10k in a new manicure robot, fires the manicurist who earns around $10k annually in commission.

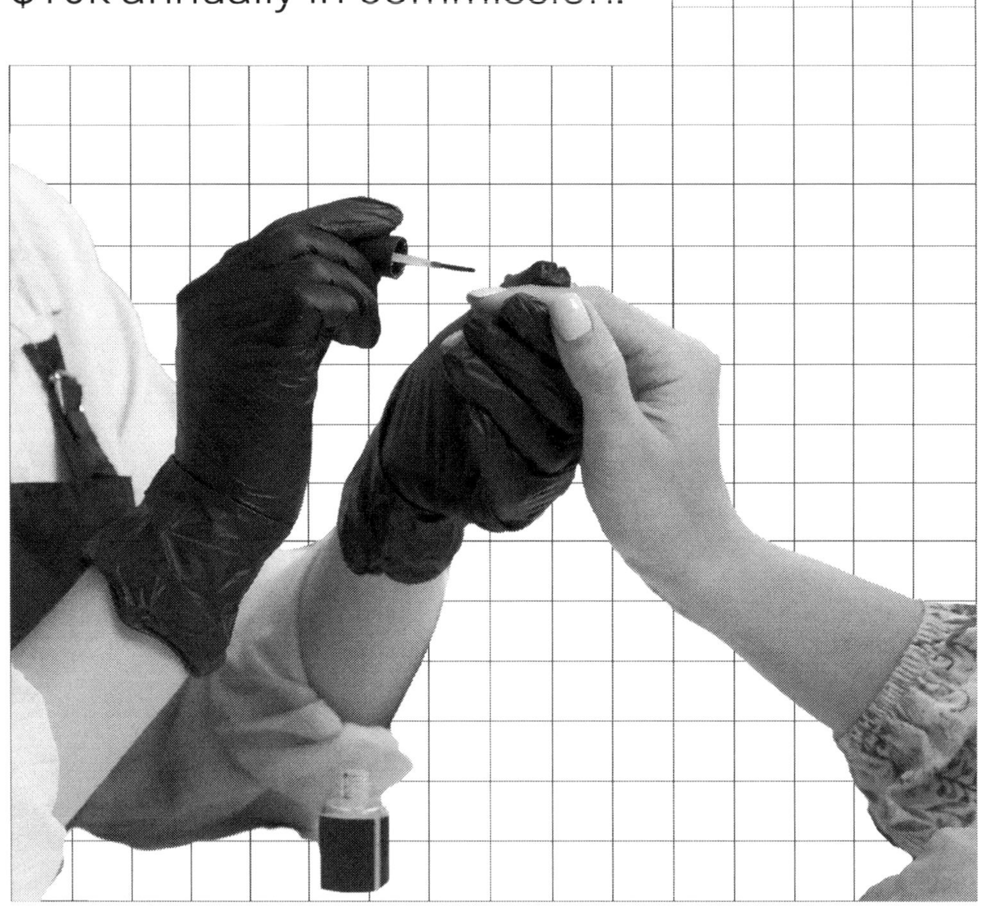

Salon Owner: Hi, I need to talk to you about something important.

Manicurist: Sure, what's on your mind?

Salon Owner: I recently made a big investment in a robot that can do manicures. It cost me $10,000, but I think it's going to revolutionize the way we do things here.

Manicurist: Wow, that sounds expensive. What does that mean for me?

Salon Owner: I'm afraid it means that I won't need you to work for me anymore. The robot can do the job faster and more efficiently than a human can, and I need to make sure I'm getting a return on my investment.

Manicurist: I understand, but this is really hard for me to hear. I barely make $10,000 a year from my commissions here.

Salon Owner: I know, and I'm sorry for any inconvenience this may cause you. I'll make sure you receive a fair severance package and assist you in finding new job opportunities.

Manicurist: Thank you, but this is going to be really tough for me. I rely on this job to make ends meet.

Salon Owner: I understand, and I wish things could be different. I value your hard work and dedication, and I'll do my best to support you during this transition.

Manicurist: I appreciate that. It's just really hard to hear that my job is being replaced by a machine.

Salon Owner: I completely understand. This was a difficult decision for me to make, but I believe it's the right one for the future of the salon. If there's anything else I can do to help, please let me know.

PROMPT A bar owner tells two bartenders that they're being replaced by robot bartenders. They ask if this applies to exotic dancers too.

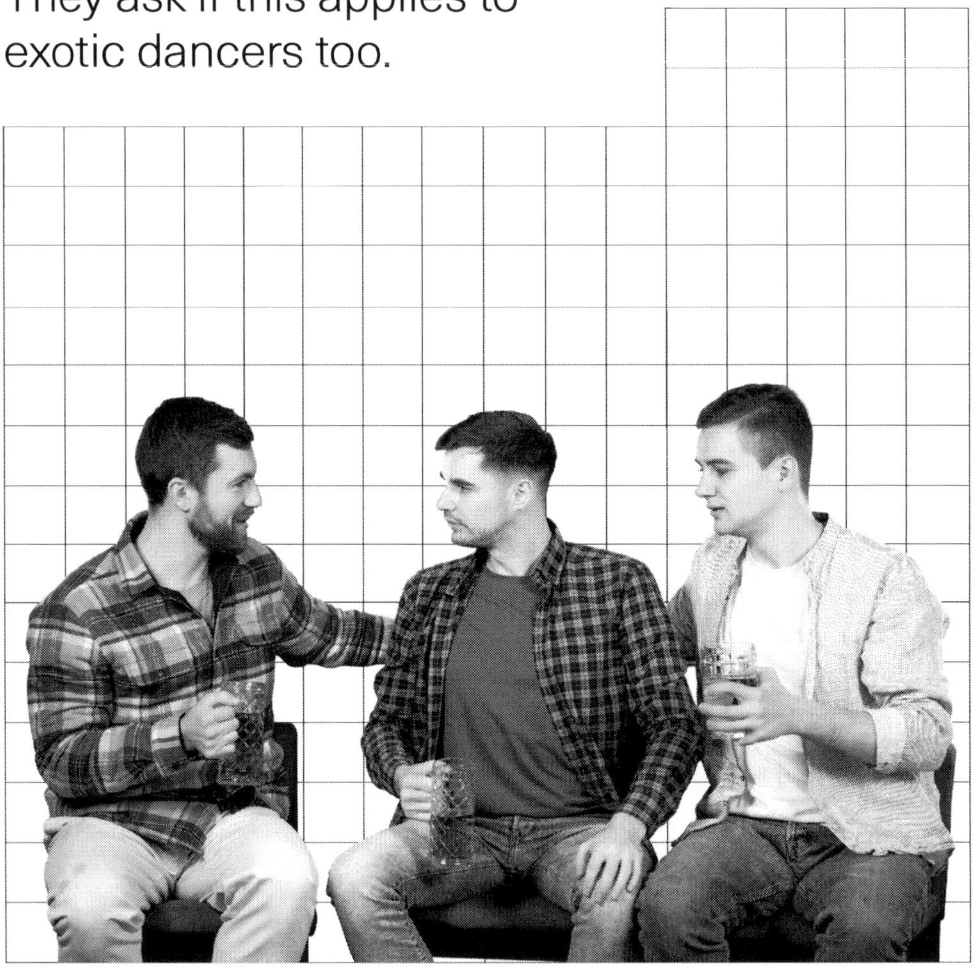

Bar Owner: Hey, can I talk to you two for a moment?

Bartender 1: Sure, what's up?

Bar Owner: I wanted to discuss the future of the bar. We've decided to introduce robot bartenders to improve efficiency and reduce costs, which means we won't need your services anymore.

Bartender 2: Wait, you're replacing us with robots?

Bar Owner: Yes, I know it's a big change, but we believe it's the right move for the business. We'll make sure you both receive a fair severance package and assist you in finding new job opportunities.

Bartender 1: That's disappointing, but we understand. Will the exotic dancers also be replaced by robots?

Bar Owner: No, the dancers' jobs are safe. The robot bartenders are meant to handle the more repetitive tasks, but we still value the human touch when it comes to entertainment.

Bartender 2: That's a relief. We'll miss working here, but we appreciate your honesty and support during this transition.

Bar Owner: Thank you both for your understanding. If you need anything during this transition, please let me know.

PROMPT Write a dialog where a Zamboni driver is told by their manager that they are getting replaced by an AI Zamboni.

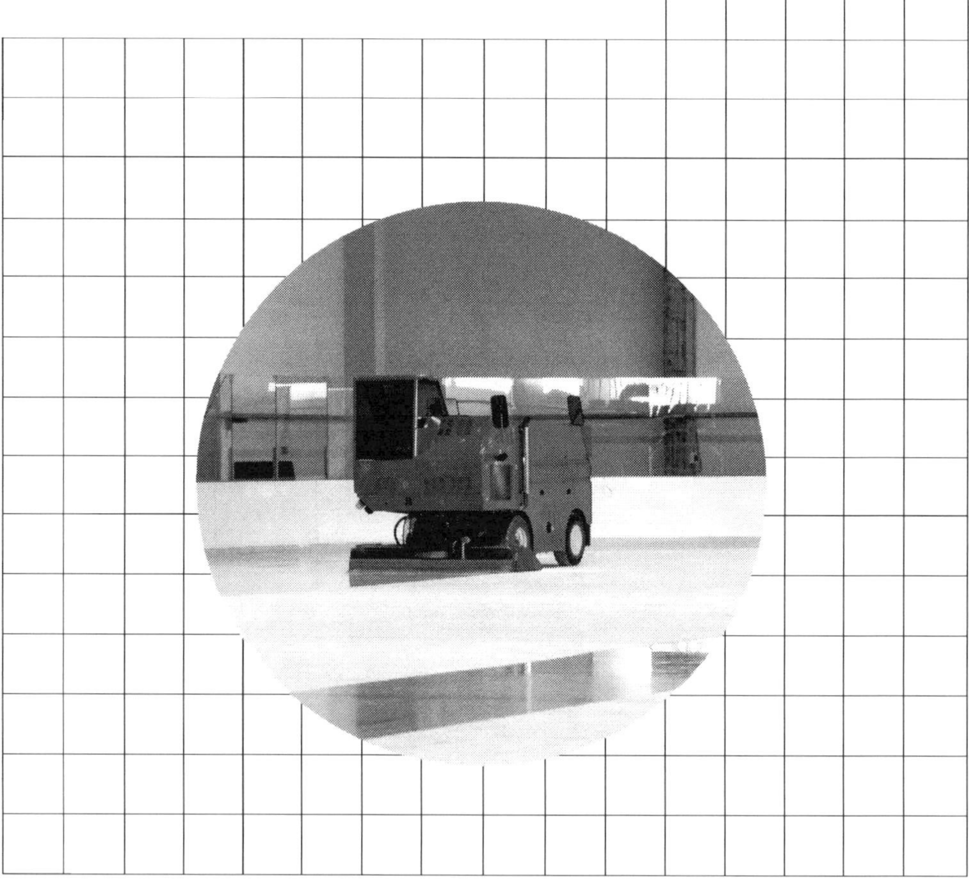

Manager: Hi there, I wanted to talk to you about some changes we're making here at the ice rink.

Zamboni driver: What kind of changes?

Manager: Well, we've decided to start using an AI Zamboni to clean the ice instead of manual Zambonis.

Zamboni driver: What does that mean for me?

Manager: Unfortunately, it means that we won't be needing your services anymore.

Zamboni driver: I don't understand, I've been working here for years. Can't I be trained to work with the new machine?

Manager: I'm sorry, but the new AI Zamboni doesn't require an operator. It can clean the ice on its own, faster and more efficiently than a manual Zamboni.

Zamboni driver: What am I supposed to do now? This was my only job.

Manager: I understand it's not easy, but we'll make sure you get a fair severance package and help you find a new job. We appreciate your dedication and hard work, and we wish you all the best in your future endeavors.

About the author

As of my last knowledge update in January 2022, I don't have specific information about an individual named Angie Waller. It's possible that she may be a private individual or someone who gained prominence after that date.

If Angie Waller is a public figure, celebrity, or someone known in a specific field, you may want to check the latest news sources, social media, or other reliable platforms for the most recent information about her. Keep in mind that the availability of information may vary, and it's always a good idea to use up-to-date sources for the latest details.

Published by
Unknown Unknowns
New York, NY
April 2024

Design:
Cover: Alexandra Ching, Field Office
Interior: Angie Waller

Special thanks:
Bill Jordan
Tara Romeo

Words written by
Angie Waller
and ChatGPT-3
Open AI

ISBN-13: 978-0-9913923-7-7
unknownunknowns.org

Unknown Unknowns is an independent imprint for books and interactive projects by Angie Waller. These works highlight ways technology has mediated the human experience.

For more information, visit UnknownUnknowns.org.